PARIS EMBASSY DIARY
1921-1922

PARIS EMBASSY DIARY 1921–1922

Agnes Blackwell Herrick
Introduced by
George G. Herrick

HAMILTON BOOKS

A member of
The Rowman & Littlefield Publishing Group
Lanham • Boulder • New York • Toronto • Plymouth, UK

Author email: GHRoque@aol.com
Copyright © 2008 by
Hamilton Books
4501 Forbes Boulevard
Suite 200
Lanham, Maryland 20706
Hamilton Books Acquisitions Department (301) 459-3366

Estover Road
Plymouth PL6 7PY
United Kingdom

All rights reserved
Printed in the United States of America
British Library Cataloging in Publication Information
Available

ISBN-13: 978-0-7618-3979-8 (paperback : alk. paper)
ISBN-10: 0-7618-3979-8 (paperback : alk. paper)

Frontispiece: Agnes Blackwell Herrick, Oil on Ivory, Marguérite Martin. 1926

∞™ The paper used in this publication meets the
minimum requirements of American National Standard
for Information Sciences—Permanence of Paper for
Printed Library Materials,
ANSI Z39.48—1984

Preface

DIARIES SOMETIMES lie forgotten in attics or closets for many years awaiting rediscovery. I must have read my grandmother Agnes Herrick's diary twenty-five years ago. In the intervening years it lived a quiet life in a box with old family photograph albums. Finding it once again after a recent move, I read it with great pleasure and had the thought of presenting a summary of it to a wider readership.

The diary runs from 15 August 1921 to 30 June 1922. It opens as Agnes has arrived in France to act as a hostess at

Preface

the Embassy in Paris where her father-in-law, Myron T. Herrick, has been appointed the American Ambassador.

Agnes Blackwell Herrick was born in Las Vegas, New Mexico on 25 October 1881. Her father, Arthur M. Blackwell, was a partner in an important general merchandising firm providing essential supplies of all kinds throughout the Southwest. He sold out his shares in 1901 and moved his family to St. Louis, where Agnes married Parmely Webb Herrick in 1906. The couple lived in Cleveland, Ohio until Agnes moved to Paris in 1921. She remained there until the Ambassador died in 1929 when she returned to Cleveland. The Herrick couple moved to New York City in 1934, where Parmely died in 1937. Agnes subsequently lived in New York City until her death in 1957.

The forty-year-old Agnes had known Paris during Herrick's first embassy

Preface

there before World War 1. Thus she knew exactly where she was headed and she was full of excitement for the adventure. The Paris years in the twenties would color her imagination for the rest of her life. She acquired a good sense of taste for dress, furnishings and *objets d'art* and, ever afterwards, her apartments seemed to have a Parisian look. A lady of style, she was petite, soft, and chic, with a gurgling sense of humor and a great capacity for friendship.

Agnes dictated almost daily entries for her diary to her French secretary. The receptacle was an ordinary loose-leaf 9 ¾ inch by 7 ¼ inch ring binder. Owing to the informality of the style and the language barrier there were many misspellings of names in the cramped, single-spaced text. The typewritten diary runs 86 pages. There was no attempt at, or time for, literary polish. There was no time because, as the diary attests, the

Preface

rhythm of daily official and social life went on at such a fast tempo.

The diary is chiefly a list of social engagements and the people she met. Although Agnes sometimes recounts what she has heard at the dinner table about political and diplomatic events, those observations are too few and too slight to record here. Altogether it presents one more first-hand picture of social and cultural life in Paris at that interesting time.

George G. Herrick
Newport, RI

Acknowledgments

I AM GRATEFUL for the helpful advice and contributions I received from Nelson W. Aldrich, my sister, Anita G. Herrick, and Elizabeth de Lyrot.

Introduction

AMERICAN AMBASSADOR Myron T. Herrick (1854-1929) landed at Le Havre, France on 14 July 1921 to rapturous official and public acclaim. His progress into Paris was all but triumphal, with a private train to Paris and a mounted escort from the Chancellery to the Elysée Palace the following day.

The former Republican Governor of Ohio had won fame during his previous ambassadorial posting to Paris from 1912-1914. During those dark days after the start of WWI, he had earned the undying friendship of the French nation.

Introduction

The story has been told in Colonel T. Bentley Mott's *Myron T. Herrick, Friend of France* (1930) and in many other records. The second American, with Benjamin Franklin, to be called *Citoyen de Paris,* he was to become the first to win the Grand Cross of the French Legion of Honor. He became something of an international figure when, in 1927, he played a conspicuous role in the reception of Charles Lindbergh after his momentous transatlantic flight to Paris.

It was a different Europe, and a different Paris, to which the Ambassador was returning. The German and Austro-Hungarian Empires had vanished, Britain had been crippled by human losses of the war, France had been shattered economically, and the map of Europe had been redrawn by the Paris Peace Conference. So great had been their losses that Frenchmen no longer wanted to dwell on the past and remem-

Introduction

ber what they wanted to forget. Instead, they looked forward to a new and liberating time.

The widowed Ambassador had asked his daughter-in-law, Agnes Herrick, to move from Cleveland, Ohio to Paris with her ten year-old son, Parmely Webb Herrick Jr., to act as official hostess at the Embassy. Her husband, Parmely Webb Herrick, would remain in Cleveland to attend to family business affairs, traveling out to France several times a year for extended visits.

Agnes had arrived in advance of the Ambassador, on 21 June, to secure lodgings for the family. She was to find temporary quarters in a cottage at Garches, near St. Cloud, just outside Paris. Before the summer was over they would establish as a residence in town the *hôtel* of the Prince Jacques de Broglie at 16 Avenue de Messine, a quiet street in the eighth arrondissement off the Boulevard

Introduction

Haussmann. It was at Garches that on 15 August she had the happy inspiration to start a diary, as a record one day for her son.

In one of the few extended passages in the diary, Agnes reflects, on 6 September 1921, about her privileged situation:

> It's a long cry from the little Western town of Las Vegas, New Mexico, that windswept and sand-blown village of the Prairies with its breadth of sky and its glorious surrounding rocks, to the fascinating brilliant Paris of today where I find myself as the daughter-in-law of the American Ambassador, placed in the most interesting and happy position imaginable.
>
> I remember so well as a child, and such a melancholy recollection it is, of listening in the small hours of the night to the trains pulling out of the little station a few blocks from our home and going, shrieking, puffing and panting,

Introduction

into the desert—it filled my soul with a longing and a very intense desire of wanting to be on that fairy express which held so much interest and fascination for me as to its destination—to be rushed away into a wonderland of new sights and sounds.

I remember the wind used to blow—it cried and moaned around the corners of the house until I was almost frantic with sadness and the feeling of helplessness.

How many years ago that was! I finally took that selfsame train, it must have been the very one that had given me the dreams and longings, and after many stages, and many years, it has landed me in Paris.

The busy round of social activities ran parallel to, in fact comprised, much of the hard work of diplomatic life. Ambassador Herrick was later to say how exhausting it had all been. Aside from the

Introduction

management of the Embassy and its correspondence with Washington D.C., there was the study and negotiation of important and difficult problems, and countless public appearances requiring appropriate remarks. It was Harold Nicolson who wrote that, "The art of diplomacy, like that of water colours, has suffered much from the fascination it exercises upon the amateur."

The main diplomatic concerns were the economic and financial reconstruction of Europe, for which Herrick's background as a banker was so pertinent, and the thorny question of German reparations for the war. Differences of opinion between the British, French, and Americans were sometimes acute. There were two important diplomatic conferences during this period, in Washington (on disarmament) and at Cannes (on German reparations). On 15 February 1922 Agnes commented that "a resort like

Introduction

Cannes will not be picked again for the Conference. Baccarat and *chemin de fer*, golf, jazz, gay dinners with jazz and half clad vamps do not go to give dignity to any dignified Commissioner." The newspapers and weeklies called it a traveling circus.

It must be remembered that Ambassadors then had to operate mostly on their own, without today's hourly communication with their Foreign Ministries. Herrick's reputation was such that when, in 1924, he needed French currency to buy a new residence for the Embassy, his known intervention in the foreign exchange market out of his own pocket caused a declining French franc to rebound. The Ambassador's dispatches on such complex and emotionally charged issues would fill volumes.

The Embassy team, assembled by Herrick, consisted of Sheldon Whitehouse as Counselor, Colonel Mott as Defense

Introduction

Attaché, Robert Woods Bliss as First Secretary, Harold H. Tittmann as Third Secretary and Laurence Norton as Private Secretary.

There were about 10,000 Americans resident in Paris at the time. The American colony was highly articulated, with many social, cultural, religious and educational institutions.

The post-War Red scare, much abhorred in certain European circles, did not spare Agnes' happy social rounds or escape the notice of her diary. As the Sacco and Vanzetti trial dragged on in Boston, an innocuous-looking package labeled "Perfume" arrived at the Embassy Residence on 19 October anonymously addressed to the Ambassador. It in fact contained a bomb, which exploded in an empty upstairs room when opened, causing some injuries to the valet, who had alertly detected the bomb and moved it there. Two years before, in April 1910,

Introduction

thirty bombs disguised as samples from a department store had been mailed to prominent Americans in the U.S., including John D. Rockefeller and J.P. Morgan.

Diplomatic life requires travel throughout the country of assignment and even abroad. Agnes records visits to Coblentz and Cologne in Germany, to Brussels, Ghent and Ypres in Belgium and to London. There are visits to Nancy, Compiègne and Chantilly in Northern France, to Normandy and Brittany in the West, to Biarritz, St. Jean de Luz and Carcassonne in the South West and all over the French Riviera. These excursions also provided time for vacation. Agnes' spare remarks nevertheless represent a contemporary response to these itineraries and enlist our appreciation.

Outside Paris, the Herricks visited the châteaux of friends, where Parmely Jr. could sometimes row in a moat. They

Introduction

golfed at St. Cloud, Monte Carlo, Cannes, Deauville, Cagnes and Fontainebleau. They went to the horse races at Chantilly. Indeed, in July 1914 the Ambassador had been sitting next to the Austro-Hungarian ambassador at the Longchamps race course on 28 June when the latter was handed a telegram announcing the assassination of Archduke Franz Ferdinand at Sarajevo.

Agnes went to the theatre over a dozen times during this year, carefully noting down the names of the plays: *Faisons Un Rêve, Claudine Est Comme Ça, Le Bonheur De Ma Femme, La Flamme*, and others. A library of books tells how important a feature of life the theatre then was in Paris. There were over forty active theatres. She went to private musicales, to revues, to the monologues of Ruth Draper, to the ballet, and to the formerly *risqué* Masked Ball at the Opéra. There was even time to

Introduction

read four books of the day, three of them in French, one of them being *La Terre Trembla* about the Russian Revolution by Claude Anet. And, of course, she read the French newspaper *Le Figaro* every day to stay up on things. It was a full cultural immersion and education.

Privately, she played bridge whenever possible with the Ambassador and friends. Bridge was popular and the rules of Contract Bridge were just being codified. Agnes marked a G or B after names in her address book to remind her who played golf or bridge. Her constant companions and closest friends on all accounts were Sheldon and Mary Whitehouse. She went to many of the premier restaurants of the day: Café Madrid, Larue, the Ritz.

Above all they danced. Most of the top restaurants offered dancing. And then there were the nightclubs: Ciro's, Zelli's on Montmartre, Acacias, the Perroquet,

Introduction

the Oh So Different, the Hôtel Meurice. Agnes and her friends danced until 3 A.M. or 4 A.M. There was a mania for dancing. The One Step, popularized before the war, was still in vogue. Agnes also attended several private balls. It was the Age of Jazz and Blues. In Michael Arlen's best-selling novel, *The Green Hat* (1924), he described Paris in 1922:

"They call this rhythm the Blues. It reminded you of regret. It reminded you of a small white face suddenly thrown back against your arm with a smile. . . . It reminded you of things you had never done with women you had never met. . . . The Lido lay like a temptation before your mind, and the songs of the gondoliers raved into the measure of whispering feet. . . . You danced again beneath the vermilion moon of Algeria, between the American Bar and the pyramid cypress tree."

During the daytime Agnes often went to the Cercle Interallié, a popular meeting

Introduction

place. She took tea with friends and admired their beautiful *hôtels particuliers*. She went shopping on the Left Bank for jade flowers and *Compagnie des Indes* china. There were excursions with young Parmely to Le Choc, a chocolatier on the Left Bank. And there were couturiers to see. And always, she needed to work on the lists of guests which "takes time and thought." Like so many others, "the *beau monde*, the *demi-monde*, brain specialists, students of psychology and the morbidly curious," she followed the sensational murder trial of Landru, who was said to have killed fifteen women, and even went to the court room on one occasion to witness emotionally charged proceedings.

In addition to the diary, Agnes left a copy of the Embassy's Dinner Party Record, 1921-1922. It preserves menus and place settings for 73 lunches and dinners. Agnes also organized teas for as many as 240 people.

Introduction

The menus make for appetizing reading and may be taken as representative of the time and place. A typical eight-course dinner consisted of soup, fish, beef, fowl, salad, vegetable, dessert, and cake, a gustatory steeplechase that would dismay all but the heartiest today. A representative menu might have been Consommé Rachel, Turbot à la Duglére, Côtelettes d'agneau petits pois, Galantine de poularde truffé, Salade de laitues cuites, Haricots verts, Pudding glacé au chocolat, and Petits gâteaux. The chef's favorite may have been the *bombe glacée*, an ice cream mixture with different flavorings disposed in concentric circle layers in a mold. Sixteen different *bombes* figure in this collection of menus, with descriptive designations such as: Javanaise, Muscovite, Alhambra and Orientale, and Cléopâtre, Africaine and Sicilienne, a sort of geography of exotic taste sensation.

Introduction

Ambassador Herrick's luncheon and dinner guests included the French aristocracy, the *beau monde*, the diplomatic corps, and senior French government and ministerial officials. WWI generals, prominent Americans in Paris, banking leaders from New York, the cultural élite, and society figures also came. He was to receive nine other ambassadors, French President Alexandre Millerand, French government ministers such as Aristide Briand and Raymond Poincaré, old WWI friends Marshall Joseph Joffre and Jules Jusserand, General Pershing, and the Shah of Persia.

The *crème de la crème* of Parisian society came to dinner: The Comtesse Greffulhe, who was the model for the Marcel Proust's Duchesse de Guermantes, was the most elegant, intelligent, fashionable, and influential *grande dame* of Paris, and friends of writers, artists, and musicians. The Belgian Prince and

Introduction

Princess de Ligne. The Duc de Gramont, whose private golf course became Le Golfe de Mortefontaine. The Marquis de Laborde, whose forbear had been banker to Louis XV. Lord Berners, "The Last Eccentric," who was portrayed as Lord Merlin in Nancy Mitford's *The Pursuit of Love*. There was a long roll call of the French nobility that echoes several centuries of French history: De Polignac, de Broglie, St. Sauveur, Faucigny-Lucinge, de la Tour d'Auvergne, Chévigné, de Noailles, de Castellane.

The most respected Americans in Paris, Walter Berry and the Walter Gays, about whom so much has been written, came often. The portraitist Philip de Laszlo and sculptors Paul Manship and Herbert Haseltine dined there. The actor Charlie Chaplin (who discussed Einstein and the Fourth Dimension with Agnes over luncheon) was a guest, as were monologist Ruth Draper, interior decorator

Introduction

Elsie de Wolfe, architect Stanford White, and musician Irving Berlin. Although not a New Yorker himself, Herrick's connections in the banking world there brought to his table many New York financial men like J.P. Morgan and George F. Baker who sought his wisdom. There was a sprinkling of Vanderbilts, Goelets and other American society figures too, many of whom had a Gilded Age association with summertime Newport, Rhode Island.

Generally, these guests were prominent or had been prominent in society or in their own field of endeavor for many years. They were at the top of the world in Paris. It was a world they had known for a long time and had naturally come to assume as their station in life and not so exceptional as to write memoirs about. The diplomats are now forgotten, but "Paris in the 1920's" lives on, labeled as a subject about talented but self-promoting young American writers, albeit with

Introduction

impressive potential, who were not at the top of the world, but thought they were. They believed everything about America was "stupid," and they even joked about the American Ambassador's efforts to raise money for a devastated France. Others simply lost themselves in an orgy of entertainment, Dadaism, and frantic artistic experimentation that fermented in Paris in 1921. It was the birth of Modernism on every front, in music, ballet, literature, and art. But their time had not yet come, and they represented only one aspect of a broader picture of which they were blissfully unaware. The antics of impecunious artists and thirsty writers of the period, amusing though they were, still hold sway today over our popular imagination instead of the professionalism and outstanding gifts of leading statesmen and diplomats, who wrestled with real problems rather than fictional or artistic ones.

Introduction

And so, Agnes fulfilled her obligation to history. She was witness to an age of refinement that would not be seen again. She was an intelligent woman with privileged access to events and to some of the principal people involved with them. What she saw was perhaps a last echo of the *Belle Epoque* and the first tremors of renewed national rivalries that contained the seeds of further struggle and the war that lay ahead. Meanwhile, the music played on and they danced the night away in the city of Paris, where cultural life was so rich and varied.

We are grateful that she recorded this for us.

Ambassador Myron T. Herrick, Oil Painting, Philip de Laszlo. 1922

The Herrick Residence, 16 Avenue de Messine

Ambassador Myron T. Herrick and his son, Parmely Webb Herrick

Agnes Blackwell Herrick, London. 1924

Parmely Webb Herrick Jr. circa 1919

Selections From the Diary

1921

Sept. 25

A GOLDEN AUTUMN DAY. We motored to Nangis to spend Sunday with Countess Greffulhe, née Caraman Chimay, at Bois Boudran, such a wonderful beautiful old château set in a perfect park of about 6,000 acres. Madame is charming and still very beautiful. After lunch we all went in a *char à banc* driven by magnificent horses—and with liveried servants to beck and call, through grand avenues of hemlocks, through beautiful *allées* of trees, and drew up at a large lake where we were to fish. Good catch we made from the set trimmers. We rowed about for an hour before going back for tea. Tea was served in a large dining room filled with beautiful tapestries and boiseries—old silver and china—quite too lovely—and such delicious goodies for tea.

At about 6 we started back to Paris and I shall never forget how beautiful the park was as we drove out. The sun was setting and all the animals came running and jumping into open spaces. Hundreds of deer, rabbits, pheasants—Parmely Jr. had such a lovely time.

Nov. 20

A gray overcast day and Sunday. Dad {the Ambassador}, Parmely Jr., and his {dog} Capi and I motored to St. Germain-en-Laye to have luncheon with Lady Michel-

Selections from the Diary

man. She has leased for 18 years the Ancien Hôtel Courtemer which is perfectly charming, having been built in 1751 by Le Nôtre. There is a delightful garden and quite near the Forest of Marly. The house Lady Michelman has done over with great taste and much comfort. The Marquis de Castellane, Mrs. Dreyfus, Lord Berners were there. After luncheon the Duchesse de Guiche came over with her four lovely boys, the grandsons of the Duc de Gramont. The children went with the pony cart to the forest, while we went to see some lovely old houses which St. Germain is full of. We saw the fascinating house and garden with its tremendously fine view of the Forest of Marly that was built by the Procureur of Louis XIII. Then the house of Madame de Montespan and a sweet old place with a pavilion that was used by Napoleon as a hunting lodge and which belonged to the Angoulême family, and which is now for sale. It is full of beautiful boisereies and has great charm, and the most lovely garden.

We went back for tea with the children and then motored to Paris. I stopped in to see Mary Whitehouse and her new baby.

At the Peace Conference {in Washington} tomorrow, {Foreign Minister Aristide} Briand will *"prendre la parole"* to expose the position of France and why she must stay armed. *"Si La France n'a jamais songé à apporter de Washington un traité, elle entend rapporter un verdict."*

Dad and I had dinner in my salon before a big fire and I have spent the evening writing letters and trying to catch up on my belated correspondence.

1922

March 15

I played golf today with Dad, Norton, and Mary Whitehouse. The country is lovely

Selections from the Diary

and everything so young and green, there were fairy blossoms on trees and bushes. I went to pay my respects with Dad on the new Italian Ambassadress, Countess Sforza. She is very nice and has two charming little children. She, however, does not impress me as a woman of the world, as the much beloved and charming Countess Bonin whose departure everyone in Paris deplores. I had tea later on in the afternoon with the Marquise de Chambrun and heard some delightful music.

This evening Dad and I dined with Herman Harjes. A most pleasant, agreeable and interesting evening. General Gouroud was there. The question arose on the importance of the press and how the French more or less failed in America for not giving the proper publication and news to correspondents of our big newspapers.

Dad has finally gotten {Prime Minister Raymond} Poincaré to see the importance and he has consented to receive once a week the representatives of the American Press.

June 18

This morning at 11:30 Dad, Parm {her husband}, and the boy and his dog started for Vallière to spend the day with the Duc and Duchesse de Gramont. They have a beautiful château and their own golf course. We lunched first and after *déjeuner* we played golf and it was just like playing in a court picture. Others came out for golf and tea, the Duc and Duchesse de Guiche, Mlle de St. Sauveur, Marquis de Laborde, Princesse de Ligne and many others. It was a heavenly day and {we} returned to town late.

June 19

Dined this evening with M. and Mme Pecci Blunt. A dinner of 100 little tables.

Selections from the Diary

During dinner Italians sang and it was quite lovely. After dinner almost 200 people came in to dance. Such a lovely old Hôtel. It was so beautifully restored and the ballroom is the finest I have ever seen in Paris. The garden is a dream of loveliness and the fireworks in the form of mountains of fire, and the green lights brought {out} all the minutest details. It was a lovely night and we walked in the garden and sat on the terrace.

June 24

Dr. Walter Rathenau, German Foreign Minister, was assassinated this morning in Berlin. Another murder by the Nationalist's secret organizations who sought revenge because Rathenau signed the Treaty of Rapallo with the Bolsheviks. This evening was the Grand Prix ball at the Opéra. It was representative of a Reception in the 18th century given by

Selections from the Diary

the Doge at Venice. The Venetian and Persian costumes were wonderful, and artists of the Comédie Française and the Opéra and many social people took part in the different *entrées* and *tableaux*. The Opéra was transformed into a Doge's palace and beautiful embroidered fabrics and banners made a wonderful setting of color and brilliancy. We had a *loge* and many people came in to see us. We made the tour, danced and supped and altogether had a most delightful evening....

June 25

Today the Grand Prix, and the weather very showery. Every sort of convenience and vehicle made its way to Longchamps. We, Dad, Parm and I, sat in the Tribune with the President and Mme Millerand, Ambassadors, Ministers and the Emperor of Annan and his entourage. A wonderful sight to see the crowds of peo-

Selections from the Diary

ple that crawled . . . through the paddocks and grounds. Mme Millerand looked charming in gray and was so gracious.

This evening we dined with Elsie de Wolfe at Versailles. Alas, it rained and, instead of dining in her lovely garden which was beautifully illuminated in spite of the rain, we dined indoors at small tables. It was a most amusing evening. Many celebrities were there, including Sorel, {Russian scene and costume designer Léon} Bakst, Irving Berlin, Elsie Ferguson, {Jascha} Heifetz (who played {(the violin} most divinely for us). . . . We danced in the Long Gallery and had a most delightful evening. Getting home at 3:00 A.M.

Bibliography

Arlen, Michael. The Green Hat (1924)
Brinnin, John Malcolm. The Third Rose, Gertrude Stein and Her World (1959)
Cowley, Malcolm. Exile's Return (1934)
Mott, T. Bentley. Myron T. Herrick, Friend of France (1930)
Muirhead, Findlay and Monmarche, Marcel. Paris and Its Environs (1921)
Rieder, William A. A Charmed Couple, The Art and Life of Walter and Matilda Gay (2000)
Roberts, Christine M. Ambassador of Peace, Myron T. Herrick's Diplomatic Career in France, 1921-1929 (M.A. Thesis 1976)
Street, Julian. Where Paris Dines (1929)

Bibliography

Vaill, Amanda. Everybody Was Young, Gerald and Sara Murphy, A Lost Generation Love Story (1998)

Watson, Bruce. Sacco and Vanzetti, The Men, the Murders and the Judgement of Mankind (2007)

Wilson, Robert Frost. Paris on Parade (1924)